Date: _____

T☀day:

Hot Stuff:

_____
_____
_____
_____
_____

Status report:

☐ Wiped out!

☐ completely satisfied!

☐ Ready for more!

How I feel today: (circle)

Date: _____

Today:

_____
_____
_____
_____
_____
_____
_____
_____
_____
_____

Hot Stuff:

_____
_____
_____
_____
_____

Status report:

☐ Wiped out!

☐ completely satisfied!

☐ Ready for more!

How I feel today: (circle)

Date: _____

T☀day:

_____
_____
_____
_____
_____
_____
_____
_____
_____
_____

Hot Stuff:

_____
_____
_____
_____
_____

Status report:

☐ Wiped out!

☐ completely satisfied!

☐ Ready for more!

How I feel today: (circle)

Date: _____

T☼day:

Hot Stuff:

_____
_____
_____
_____
_____

Status report:

- ☐ Wiped out!
- ☐ completely satisfied!
- ☐ Ready for more!

How I feel today: (circle)

Date: _____

T☼day:

_____
_____
_____
_____
_____
_____
_____
_____
_____
_____

Hot Stuff:

_____
_____
_____
_____
_____

Status report:

☐ Wiped out!

☐ completely satisfied!

☐ Ready for more!

How I feel today: (circle)

Date: _____

TOday:

_____
_____
_____
_____
_____
_____
_____
_____
_____
_____

Hot Stuff:

_____
_____
_____
_____
_____

Status report:

☐ Wiped out!

☐ completely satisfied!

☐ Ready for more!

How I feel today: (circle)

Date: _____

TOday:

_____
_____
_____
_____
_____
_____
_____
_____
_____

Hot Stuff:

_____
_____
_____
_____
_____

Status report:

☐ Wiped out!

☐ completely satisfied!

☐ Ready for more!

How I feel today: (circle)

Date: _____

TODAY:

_____
_____
_____
_____
_____
_____
_____
_____
_____
_____

Hot Stuff:

_____
_____
_____
_____
_____

Status report:

☐ Wiped out!

☐ completely satisfied!

☐ Ready for more!

How I feel today: (circle)

Date: _____

T:O:day:

Hot Stuff:

_____
_____
_____
_____
_____

Status report:

☐ **Wiped out!**

☐ **completely satisfied!**

☐ **Ready for more!**

How I feel today: (circle)

Date: _____

TODAY:

_____
_____
_____
_____
_____
_____
_____
_____
_____

Hot Stuff:

_____
_____
_____
_____

Status report:

☐ Wiped out!

☐ completely satisfied!

☐ Ready for more!

How I feel today: (circle)

Date: _____

TОday:

_____
_____
_____
_____
_____
_____
_____
_____
_____

Hot Stuff:

_____
_____
_____
_____
_____

Status report:

☐ Wiped out!

☐ completely satisfied!

☐ Ready for more!

How I feel today: (circle)

Date: _____

TODAY:

_____
_____
_____
_____
_____
_____
_____
_____
_____
_____

Hot Stuff:

_____
_____
_____
_____
_____

Status report:

☐ Wiped out!

☐ completely satisfied!

☐ Ready for more!

How I feel today: (circle)

Date: _____

Today:

Hot Stuff:

_____
_____
_____
_____
_____
_____
_____

Status report:

☐ Wiped out!

☐ completely satisfied!

☐ Ready for more!

How I feel today: (circle)

Date: _____

T☀day:

Hot Stuff:

_____
_____
_____
_____
_____
_____
_____
_____
_____
_____

_____
_____
_____
_____
_____

Status report:

☐ Wiped out!

☐ completely satisfied!

☐ Ready for more!

How I feel today: (circle)

Date: _____

T☼day:

Hot Stuff:

_____
_____
_____
_____
_____
_____
_____
_____
_____
_____

_____
_____
_____
_____
_____
_____

Status report:

- ☐ Wiped out!
- ☐ completely satisfied!
- ☐ Ready for more!

How I feel today: (circle)

Date: _____

To day:

_____
_____
_____
_____
_____
_____
_____
_____
_____
_____
_____

Hot Stuff:

_____
_____
_____
_____

Status report:

☐ **Wiped out!**

☐ **completely satisfied!**

☐ **Ready for more!**

How I feel today: (circle)

Date: _____

TOday:

_____
_____
_____
_____
_____
_____
_____
_____
_____

Hot StuFf:

_____
_____
_____
_____
_____

Status report:

☐ Wiped out!

☐ completely satisfied!

☐ Ready for more!

How I feel today: (circle)

Date: _____

T☼day:

Hot Stuff:

_____
_____
_____
_____
_____
_____

Status report:

- ☐ **Wiped out!**
- ☐ **completely satisfied!**
- ☐ **Ready for more!**

How I feel today: (circle)

Date: _____

TODAY:

_____
_____
_____
_____
_____
_____
_____
_____
_____
_____
_____
_____

Hot Stuff:

_____
_____
_____
_____
_____
_____

Status report:

☐ **Wiped out!**

☐ **completely satisfied!**

☐ **Ready for more!**

How I feel today: (circle)

Date: _____

TODay:

_____
_____
_____
_____
_____
_____
_____
_____
_____
_____

Hot Stuff:

_____
_____
_____
_____

Status report:

☐ Wiped out!

☐ completely satisfied!

☐ Ready for more!

How I feel today: (circle)

Date: _____

T☼day:

Hot Stuff:

_____

_____

_____

_____

_____

Status report:

☐ **Wiped out!**

☐ **completely satisfied!**

☐ **Ready for more!**

How I feel today: (circle)

Date: _____

TODAY:

_____
_____
_____
_____
_____
_____
_____
_____
_____
_____

Hot Stuff:

_____
_____
_____
_____

Status report:

- ☐ Wiped out!
- ☐ completely satisfied!
- ☐ Ready for more!

How I feel today: (circle)

Date: _____

TODAY:

_____
_____
_____
_____
_____
_____
_____
_____
_____
_____

Hot Stuff:

_____
_____
_____
_____
_____

Status report:

☐ Wiped out!

☐ completely satisfied!

☐ Ready for more!

How I feel today: (circle)

Date: _____

T☀day:

_____
_____
_____
_____
_____
_____
_____
_____
_____
_____

Hot Stuff:

_____
_____
_____
_____
_____

Status report:

☐ Wiped out!

☐ completely satisfied!

☐ Ready for more!

How I feel today: (circle)

Date: _____

Today:

_____
_____
_____
_____
_____
_____
_____
_____
_____
_____

Hot Stuff:

_____
_____
_____
_____
_____

Status report:

☐ **Wiped out!**

☐ **completely satisfied!**

☐ **Ready for more!**

How I feel today: (circle)

Date: _____

TOday:

Hot Stuff:

_____
_____
_____
_____
_____
_____
_____
_____
_____
_____

_____
_____
_____
_____
_____

Status report:

☐ Wiped out!

☐ completely satisfied!

☐ Ready for more!

How I feel today: (circle)

Date: _____

Today:

_____
_____
_____
_____
_____
_____
_____
_____
_____
_____

Hot Stuff:

_____
_____
_____
_____
_____

Status report:

☐ Wiped out!

☐ completely satisfied!

☐ Ready for more!

How I feel today: (circle)

Date: _____

Today:

_____
_____
_____
_____
_____
_____
_____
_____
_____

Hot Stuff:

_____
_____
_____
_____
_____

Status report:

☐ **Wiped out!**

☐ **completely satisfied!**

☐ **Ready for more!**

How I feel today: (circle)

Date: _____

TODAY:

_____
_____
_____
_____
_____
_____
_____
_____
_____
_____
_____

Hot Stuff:

_____
_____
_____
_____

Status report:

☐ **Wiped out!**

☐ **completely satisfied!**

☐ **Ready for more!**

How I feel today: (circle)

Date: _____

Today:

Hot Stuff:

_____
_____
_____
_____
_____

Status report:

☐ **Wiped out!**

☐ **completely satisfied!**

☐ **Ready for more!**

How I feel today: (circle)

Date: _____

TODAY:

_____
_____
_____
_____
_____
_____
_____
_____
_____
_____
_____

Hot Stuff:

_____
_____
_____
_____

Status report:

☐ **Wiped out!**

☐ **completely satisfied!**

☐ **Ready for more!**

How I feel today: (circle)

Date: _____

T☼day:

Hot Stuff:

_____
_____
_____
_____
_____
_____
_____
_____
_____
_____

_____
_____
_____
_____
_____
_____

Status report:

☐ **Wiped out!**

☐ **completely satisfied!**

☐ **Ready for more!**

How I feel today: (circle)

Date: _____

TODAY:

_____
_____
_____
_____
_____
_____
_____
_____
_____

Hot Stuff:

_____
_____
_____
_____
_____

Status report:

☐ Wiped out!

☐ completely satisfied!

☐ Ready for more!

How I feel today: (circle)

Date: _____

T☼day:

Hot Stuff:

_____

_____

_____

_____

_____

_____

_____

_____

_____

_____

_____

_____

Status report:

☐ Wiped out!

☐ completely satisfied!

☐ Ready for more!

How I feel today: (circle)

Date: _____

Today:

_____
_____
_____
_____
_____
_____
_____
_____
_____

Hot Stuff:

_____
_____
_____
_____
_____
_____

Status report:

☐ **Wiped out!**

☐ **completely satisfied!**

☐ **Ready for more!**

How I feel today: (circle)

Date: _____

TODAY:

_____
_____
_____
_____
_____
_____
_____
_____
_____
_____

Hot Stuff:

_____
_____
_____
_____
_____

Status report:

☐ Wiped out!

☐ completely satisfied!

☐ Ready for more!

How I feel today: (circle)

Date: _____

T☼day:

_____
_____
_____
_____
_____
_____
_____
_____
_____
_____
_____
_____

Hot Stuff:

_____
_____
_____
_____
_____

Status report:

☐ **Wiped out!**

☐ **completely satisfied!**

☐ **Ready for more!**

How I feel today: (circle)

Date: _____

T☼day:

_____
_____
_____
_____
_____
_____
_____
_____
_____
_____

Hot Stuff:

_____
_____
_____
_____

Status report:

☐ **Wiped out!**

☐ **completely satisfied!**

☐ **Ready for more!**

How I feel today: (circle)

Date: _____

T☼day:

_____
_____
_____
_____
_____
_____
_____
_____
_____
_____
_____

Hot Stuff:

_____
_____
_____
_____
_____

Status report:

☐ **Wiped out!**

☐ **completely satisfied!**

☐ **Ready for more!**

How I feel today: (circle)

Date: _____

TODAY:

_____
_____
_____
_____
_____
_____
_____
_____
_____
_____

Hot Stuff:

_____
_____
_____
_____

Status report:

☐ **Wiped out!**

☐ **completely satisfied!**

☐ **Ready for more!**

How I feel today: (circle)

Date: _____

T☼day:

_____
_____
_____
_____
_____
_____
_____
_____
_____
_____

Hot Stuff:

_____
_____
_____
_____
_____

Status report:

☐ **Wiped out!**

☐ **completely satisfied!**

☐ **Ready for more!**

How I feel today: (circle)

Date: _____

T☼day:

Hot Stuff:

_____
_____
_____
_____
_____
_____
_____
_____

Status report:

☐ Wiped out!

☐ completely satisfied!

☐ Ready for more!

How I feel today: (circle)

Date: _____

Today:

_____
_____
_____
_____
_____
_____
_____
_____
_____
_____

Hot Stuff:

_____
_____
_____
_____
_____

Status report:

☐ Wiped out!

☐ completely satisfied!

☐ Ready for more!

How I feel today: (circle)

Date: _____

TOday:

_____
_____
_____
_____
_____
_____
_____
_____
_____

Hot Stuff:

_____
_____
_____
_____
_____

Status report:

☐ **Wiped out!**

☐ **completely satisfied!**

☐ **Ready for more!**

How I feel today: (circle)

Date: _____

TODAY:

_____
_____
_____
_____
_____
_____
_____
_____
_____
_____

Hot Stuff:

_____
_____
_____
_____
_____

Status report:

☐ Wiped out!

☐ completely satisfied!

☐ Ready for more!

How I feel today: (circle)

Date: _____

TOday:

_____
_____
_____
_____
_____
_____
_____
_____
_____
_____

Hot Stuff!

_____
_____
_____
_____

Status report:

☐ **Wiped out!**

☐ **completely satisfied!**

☐ **Ready for more!**

How I feel today: (circle)

Date: _____

T☀day:

Hot Stuff:

_____
_____
_____
_____
_____
_____
_____
_____
_____

_____
_____
_____
_____
_____

Status report:

☐ Wiped out!

☐ completely satisfied!

☐ Ready for more!

How I feel today: (circle)

Date: _____

T☼day:

Hot Stuff:

_____

_____

_____

_____

_____

_____

_____

_____

_____

_____

_____

_____

_____

_____

Status report:

☐ Wiped out!

☐ completely satisfied!

☐ Ready for more!

How I feel today: (circle)

Date: _____

T☉day:

Hot Stuff:

Status report:

☐ **Wiped out!**

☐ **completely satisfied!**

☐ **Ready for more!**

How I feel today: (circle)

Date: _____

Today:

_____
_____
_____
_____
_____
_____
_____
_____
_____
_____

Hot Stuff:

_____
_____
_____
_____

Status report:

☐ Wiped out!

☐ completely satisfied!

☐ Ready for more!

How I feel today: (circle)

Date: _____

Today:

Hot
Stuff:

Status report:

☐ Wiped out!

☐ completely satisfied!

☐ Ready for more!

How I feel today: (circle)

Date: _____

T☉day:

Hot Stuff:

_____
_____
_____
_____
_____
_____
_____
_____
_____

_____
_____
_____
_____
_____
_____

Status report:

☐ **Wiped out!**

☐ **completely satisfied!**

☐ **Ready for more!**

How I feel today: (circle)

Date: _____

T☼day:

Hot Stuff:

_____
_____
_____
_____
_____
_____

Status report:

☐ **Wiped out!**

☐ **completely satisfied!**

☐ **Ready for more!**

How I feel today: (circle)

Date: _____

Today:

_____
_____
_____
_____
_____
_____
_____
_____
_____
_____
_____

Hot Stuff:

_____
_____
_____
_____

Status report:

☐ Wiped out!

☐ completely satisfied!

☐ Ready for more!

How I feel today: (circle)

Date: _____

TODay:

_____
_____
_____
_____
_____
_____
_____
_____
_____
_____
_____
_____

Hot Stuff:

_____
_____
_____
_____
_____

Status report:

☐ Wiped out!

☐ completely satisfied!

☐ Ready for more!

How I feel today: (circle)

Date: _____

TODAY:

_____
_____
_____
_____
_____
_____
_____
_____
_____
_____

Hot Stuff:

_____
_____
_____
_____
_____

Status report:

☐ **Wiped out!**

☐ **completely satisfied!**

☐ **Ready for more!**

How I feel today: (circle)

Date: _____

Today:

_____
_____
_____
_____
_____
_____
_____
_____
_____
_____

Hot Stuff:

_____
_____
_____
_____

Status report:

- ☐ Wiped out!
- ☐ completely satisfied!
- ☐ Ready for more!

How I feel today: (circle)

Date: _____

T☀day:

_____
_____
_____
_____
_____
_____
_____
_____
_____
_____

Hot Stuff:

_____
_____
_____
_____
_____

Status report:

☐ Wiped out!

☐ completely satisfied!

☐ Ready for more!

How I feel today: (circle)

Date: _____

Today:

_____
_____
_____
_____
_____
_____
_____
_____
_____

Hot Stuff:

_____
_____
_____
_____
_____

Status report:

☐ Wiped out!

☐ completely satisfied!

☐ Ready for more!

How I feel today: (circle)

Date: _____

TODay:

_____
_____
_____
_____
_____
_____
_____
_____
_____

Hot Stuff:

_____
_____
_____
_____

Status report:

☐ **Wiped out!**

☐ **completely satisfied!**

☐ **Ready for more!**

How I feel today: (circle)

Date: _____

Today:

_____
_____
_____
_____
_____
_____
_____
_____
_____
_____

Hot Stuff:

_____
_____
_____
_____
_____
_____

Status report:

☐ Wiped out!

☐ completely satisfied!

☐ Ready for more!

How I feel today: (circle)

Date: _____

Today:

_____
_____
_____
_____
_____
_____
_____
_____
_____
_____

Hot Stuff:

_____
_____
_____
_____
_____

Status report:

☐ Wiped out!

☐ completely satisfied!

☐ Ready for more!

How I feel today: (circle)

Date: _____

TODAY:

_____
_____
_____
_____
_____
_____
_____
_____
_____
_____

Hot Stuff:

_____
_____
_____
_____

Status report:

☐ **Wiped out!**

☐ **completely satisfied!**

☐ **Ready for more!**

How I feel today: (circle)

Date: _____

T☼day:

_____
_____
_____
_____
_____
_____
_____
_____
_____
_____
_____

Hot Stuff:

_____
_____
_____
_____
_____

Status report:

- ☐ Wiped out!
- ☐ completely satisfied!
- ☐ Ready for more!

How I feel today: (circle)

Date: _____

Today:

_____
_____
_____
_____
_____
_____
_____
_____
_____
_____

Hot Stuff:

_____
_____
_____
_____
_____

Status report:

☐ Wiped out!

☐ completely satisfied!

☐ Ready for more!

How I feel today: (circle)

Date: _____

TODAY:

_____
_____
_____
_____
_____
_____
_____
_____
_____
_____
_____

Hot Stuff:

_____
_____
_____
_____

Status report:

☐ Wiped out!

☐ completely satisfied!

☐ Ready for more!

How I feel today: (circle)

Date: _____

Today:

_____
_____
_____
_____
_____
_____
_____
_____
_____

Hot Stuff:

_____
_____
_____
_____

Status report:

☐ **Wiped out!**

☐ **completely satisfied!**

☐ **Ready for more!**

How I feel today: (circle)

Date: _____

T☼day:

Hot Stuff:

_____

_____

_____

_____

_____

_____

_____

_____

_____

_____

_____

Status report:

☐ **Wiped out!**

☐ **completely satisfied!**

☐ **Ready for more!**

How I feel today: (circle)

Date: _____

T☼day:

Hot Stuff:

_____
_____
_____
_____
_____
_____

Status report:

☐ **Wiped out!**

☐ **completely satisfied!**

☐ **Ready for more!**

How I feel today: (circle)

Date: _____

TOday:

_____
_____
_____
_____
_____
_____
_____
_____
_____

Hot Stuff:

_____
_____
_____
_____
_____

Status report:

☐ Wiped out!

☐ completely satisfied!

☐ Ready for more!

How I feel today: (circle)

Date: _____

T☀day:

Hot Stuff:

_____
_____
_____
_____
_____
_____
_____
_____
_____
_____
_____

_____
_____
_____
_____
_____

Status report:

☐ Wiped out!

☐ completely satisfied!

☐ Ready for more!

How I feel today: (circle)

Date: _____

TODAY:

_____
_____
_____
_____
_____
_____
_____
_____
_____
_____
_____

Hot Stuff:

_____
_____
_____
_____
_____

Status report:

☐ Wiped out!

☐ completely satisfied!

☐ Ready for more!

How I feel today: (circle)

Date: _____

Today:

_____
_____
_____
_____
_____
_____
_____
_____
_____
_____
_____

Hot Stuff:

_____
_____
_____
_____
_____

Status report:

☐ **Wiped out!**

☐ **completely satisfied!**

☐ **Ready for more!**

How I feel today: (circle)

Date: _____

T☀day:

_____
_____
_____
_____
_____
_____
_____
_____
_____

Hot Stuff:

_____
_____
_____
_____
_____

Status report:

☐ **Wiped out!**

☐ **completely satisfied!**

☐ **Ready for more!**

How I feel today: (circle)

Date: _____

TODay:

_____
_____
_____
_____
_____
_____
_____
_____
_____
_____
_____

Hot Stuff:

_____
_____
_____
_____
_____

Status report:

☐ **Wiped out!**

☐ **completely satisfied!**

☐ **Ready for more!**

How I feel today: (circle)

Date: _____

T☼day:

Hot Stuff:

_____
_____
_____
_____
_____
_____
_____
_____
_____

_____
_____
_____
_____
_____

Status report:

☐ Wiped out!

☐ completely satisfied!

☐ Ready for more!

How I feel today: (circle)

Date: _____

T☼day:

_____
_____
_____
_____
_____
_____
_____
_____
_____
_____

Hot Stuff:

_____
_____
_____
_____
_____
_____

Status report:

☐ Wiped out!

☐ completely satisfied!

☐ Ready for more!

How I feel today: (circle)

Date: _____

T☀day:

_____
_____
_____
_____
_____
_____
_____
_____
_____
_____

Hot Stuff:

_____
_____
_____
_____

Status report:

☐ **Wiped out!**

☐ **completely satisfied!**

☐ **Ready for more!**

How I feel today: (circle)

Date: _____

T☼day:

Hot Stuff:

_____
_____
_____
_____
_____
_____
_____
_____
_____
_____

Status report:

☐ **Wiped out!**

☐ **completely satisfied!**

☐ **Ready for more!**

How I feel today: (circle)

Date: _____

Today:

_____
_____
_____
_____
_____
_____
_____
_____
_____
_____

Hot Stuff:

_____
_____
_____
_____
_____

Status report:

- [ ] Wiped out!
- [ ] completely satisfied!
- [ ] Ready for more!

How I feel today: (circle)

Date: _____

TOday:

Hot Stuff:

_____
_____
_____
_____
_____
_____

Status report:

- ☐ **Wiped out!**
- ☐ **completely satisfied!**
- ☐ **Ready for more!**

How I feel today: (circle)

Date: _____

Today:

_____
_____
_____
_____
_____
_____
_____
_____
_____
_____
_____

Hot Stuff:

_____
_____
_____ /
_____
_____

Status report:

☐ **Wiped out!**

☐ **completely satisfied!**

☐ **Ready for more!**

How I feel today: (circle)

Date: _____

TODAY:

_____
_____
_____
_____
_____
_____
_____
_____
_____
_____

Hot Stuff:

_____
_____
_____
_____
_____

Status report:

☐ Wiped out!

☐ completely satisfied!

☐ Ready for more!

How I feel today: (circle)

Date: _____

TODAY:

_____
_____
_____
_____
_____
_____
_____
_____
_____
_____

Hot Stuff:

_____
_____
_____
_____

Status report:

☐ **Wiped out!**

☐ **completely satisfied!**

☐ **Ready for more!**

How I feel today: (circle)

Date: _____

T☼day:

Hot Stuff:

_____

_____

_____

_____

_____

Status report:

☐ **Wiped out!**

☐ **completely satisfied!**

☐ **Ready for more!**

How I feel today: (circle)

Date: _____

TOday:

_____
_____
_____
_____
_____
_____
_____
_____
_____
_____

Hot StuFf:

_____
_____
_____
_____
_____

Status report:

☐ Wiped out!

☐ completely satisfied!

☐ Ready for more!

How I feel today: (circle)

Date: _____

T☼day:

Hot Stuff:

_____
_____
_____
_____
_____
_____
_____
_____
_____
_____

_____
_____
_____
_____
_____

Status report:

☐ Wiped out!

☐ completely satisfied!

☐ Ready for more!

How I feel today: (circle)

Date: _____

T☼day:

Hot Stuff:

_____
_____
_____
_____
_____

_____
_____
_____
_____

Status report:

☐ Wiped out!

☐ completely satisfied!

☐ Ready for more!

How I feel today: (circle)

Date: _____

TODAY:

_____
_____
_____
_____
_____
_____
_____
_____
_____
_____

Hot Stuff:

_____
_____
_____
_____
_____
_____

Status report:

☐ Wiped out!

☐ completely satisfied!

☐ Ready for more!

How I feel today: (circle)

Date: _____

Today:

_____
_____
_____
_____
_____
_____
_____
_____
_____
_____

Hot Stuff:

_____
_____
_____
_____
_____

Status report:

☐ **Wiped out!**

☐ **completely satisfied!**

☐ **Ready for more!**

How I feel today: (circle)

Date: _____

TOday:

_____
_____
_____
_____
_____
_____
_____
_____
_____
_____

Hot Stuff:

_____
_____
_____
_____
_____
_____

Status report:

☐ **Wiped out!**

☐ **completely satisfied!**

☐ **Ready for more!**

How I feel today: (circle)

Date: _____

TOday:

_____
_____
_____
_____
_____
_____
_____
_____
_____
_____

Hot Stuff:

_____
_____
_____
_____
_____

Status report:

☐ **Wiped out!**

☐ **completely satisfied!**

☐ **Ready for more!**

How I feel today: (circle)

Date: _____

TODAY:

_____
_____
_____
_____
_____
_____
_____
_____
_____

Hot Stuff:

_____
_____
_____
_____
_____

Status report:

☐ Wiped out!

☐ completely satisfied!

☐ Ready for more!

How I feel today: (circle)

Date: _____

T☼day:

Hot Stuff:

_____
_____
_____
_____
_____
_____
_____
_____

_____
_____
_____
_____
_____
_____

Status report:

☐ **Wiped out!**

☐ **completely satisfied!**

☐ **Ready for more!**

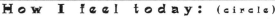
How I feel today: (circle)

Date: _____

Today:

_____
_____
_____
_____
_____
_____
_____
_____
_____
_____

Hot Stuff:

_____
_____
_____
_____
_____

Status report:

☐ Wiped out!

☐ completely satisfied!

☐ Ready for more!

How I feel today: (circle)

Date: _____

Today:

_____
_____
_____
_____
_____
_____
_____
_____
_____
_____

Hot Stuff:

_____
_____
_____
_____
_____

Status report:

☐ **Wiped out!**

☐ **completely satisfied!**

☐ **Ready for more!**

How I feel today: (circle)